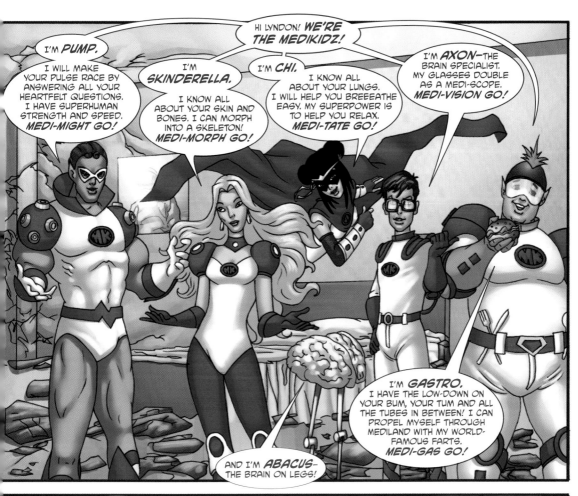

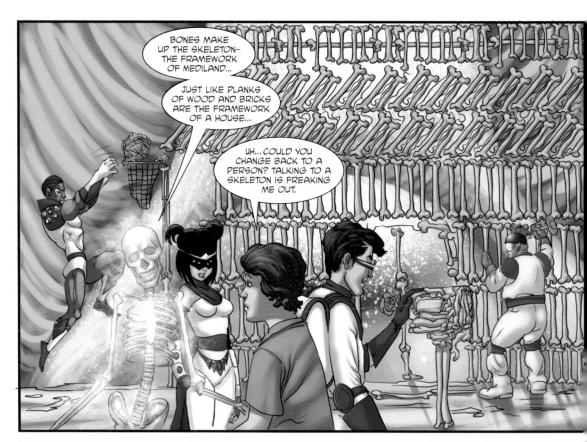

SOME BONES ARE DESIGNED TO *PROTECT* THE BODY'S ORGANS FROM BEING SQUASHED...

IMPORTANT THINGS NEED TO GO IN A CASE...

JUST LIKE YOUR LUNCH.

MY BRAIN IS SO IMPORTANT I SHOULD HAVE *TWO* SKULLS TO PROTECT IT.

I THINK YOUR *ONE* SKULL IS THICK ENOUGH.

BONES SEEM LIKE THEY ARE 'ROCK SOLID' FROM THE *OUTSIDE.*

THWACK... THWACK...

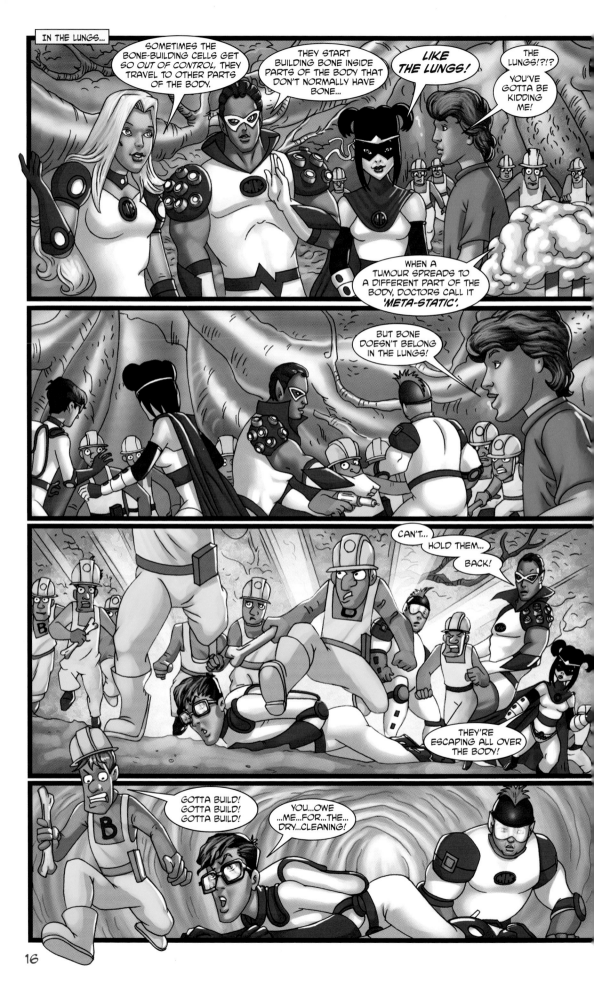

20

29